Resolving CloudFormation Stack Creation Failure

Table of Contents

Chapter 1. Introduction

In this Special Report, we delve into the technical landscape of "Resolving CloudFormation Stack Creation Failure", a rather complex but utterly crucial subject matter, especially for those absorbed in the realm of cloud computing. Fear not, however, as this report is compiled to give you a comprehensive understanding in the most practical and intimate way possible. It has been carefully curated not to mystify but to elucidate, to decode the intricate topic in a thoroughly down-to-earth tone, making it accessible to professionals of all calibers. Here, we lay out the common challenges faced, expert-tested strategies to rectify them, and innovative practices to prevent similar issues in the future. This Special Report becomes your guiding hand, aiding you to navigate through the technical labyrinth of CloudFormation without breaking a sweat.

Chapter 2. Understanding CloudFormation and Stack Creation

Admittedly, to fully grasp and handle the issues of CloudFormation Stack Creation Failure, it becomes fundamentally necessary to understand the core nomenclature, CloudFormation, and the concept of Stack Creation. In this section, we walk you through the cornerstone of our topic.

CloudFormation, an integral service provided by AWS (Amazon Web Services), allows users to describe and set up all the AWS resources so that you can spend less time managing those resources, and more time focusing on your applications running atop.

In the simplest of terms, the term 'stack' in CloudFormation equates to a set of AWS resources created and managed as a single unit. Thus, when these stacks are created, modified, or deleted, it occurs collectively, ensuring consistent and predictable infrastructural state.

2.1. Anatomy of a CloudFormation Template

A CloudFormation template is a JSON or YAML format text file. This serialized document defines the AWS resources and properties necessary for your application stack. To be leveraged effectively, it contains four main elements. Let's take a brief look at these components.

1. `AWSTemplateFormatVersion`: The AWS CloudFormation template version which you want to use; a great optional parameter that controls the specific behavior of some templates.

2. `Description`: A text string description of the template; it is best practice to provide detailed information here for documentation purposes.

3. `Resources`: Under this header, you define all the necessary AWS resources that you want to create and configure.

4. `Outputs`: This section allows you to output values; for instance, the value of an Amazon RDS Database Instance address after it's created.

The Template Resource Types available are defined by AWS and represent the different resources that you can manage using CloudFormation.

2.2. Creating a Stack

Stack creation is a multi-step process. Having a handle on this process can save you valuable time debugging potential failures.

1. Create a CloudFormation template: Design your stack on paper, noting which resources need to interact with one another. This becomes your template blueprint. You then implement this in JSON or YAML.

2. Validate your template: CloudFormation has a built-in feature to validate templates before they are used in stack creation. Here, syntax errors and some semantic errors are caught before deployment stage.

3. Create and manage the stack: After successful validation, you can launch your stack using the AWS Management Console, AWS CLI, or CloudFormation APIs.

4. Monitor stack creation and debugging if necessary: View the stack creation progress in the CloudFormation console; if the stack creation fails, refer to stack events to identify the resource failings.

2.3. From Template to Stack

Templates become stacks through the process of creation tasks performed by AWS CloudFormation. This process includes creating and provisioning each declared resource in the template, monitoring the combined status of these resource creations, and finally declaring the stack creation a success or diagnosing failures.

During the process, AWS CloudFormation reports real-time data back to you via stack events. Stack events are timestamped activities carried out on a stack or individual resources within that stack. They can be invaluable for understanding the flow of events during stack creation, particularly if your stack fails to create.

2.4. Common Errors During Stack Creation

As you embark on the journey of Stack Creation, here are some common pitfalls to be aware of.

1. YAML Formatting issues: YAML syntax requires specific space formatting and can be quite sensitive.

2. Circular Dependency: This happens when AWS resources depend on each other in a closed loop, thereby preventing the creation or deletion of resources in the necessary order.

3. Unavailable Resources: Certain AWS resource types may not be available in all regions or accounts.

4. Permissions and Policy Issues: Permission issues like not having appropriate access to the required AWS resources can lead to failed stack creation.

Understanding these common errors can streamline your stack creation process, reducing failure rates, and bettering your

CloudFormation experience. Remember, the mastery of managing CloudFormation Stack Creation Failure starts with getting the basics right, and that's exactly what this section was all about.

This ends our extensive journey through the basic understanding of CloudFormation and Stack Creation. The next time a CloudFormation template is in your hands, or a Stack Creation is on the horizon, you'll know your way around it with increased confidence and precision.

Chapter 3. Identifying CloudFormation Stack Creation Failures

As we delve into the technicalities of CloudFormation Stack Creation Failures, the first step requires a clear understanding of what exactly these failures are. CloudFormation stack failures essentially boil down to unsuccessful attempts at creating, updating, or deleting a stack. The crux of these failures can revolve around template validation errors, insufficient permissions, or resource constraint issues.

3.1. Recognizing CloudFormation Stack Failures

When a stack fails, AWS CloudFormation™ informs you by changing the stack status to `ROLLBACK_COMPLETE` or `ROLLBACK_FAILED`. Many a time, the console elucidates an error message alongside, making it easier for you to fathom the root cause. The Error Message field in the Events tab is rendered in an easy-to-understand manner, elucidating in brief the cause behind the failure. More comprehensive information can be found in Error Message details. If a rollback is initiated for any reason, it's essential to know that it doesn't impact any successfully created resources outside of the stack's operation.

3.2. Digging Deeper into Error Messages

Error messages found in the Events tab or Stack events in AWS CloudFormation console often hold vital clues to understanding the cause of failure. Different types of errors can occur, such as syntax errors, unsupported property errors, resource property conflicts, and more.

Let's break down some common types of error messages:

- Resource Not Ready: The specified resource couldn't be created within the timeout duration. Resolving this can often involve examining other dependencies of the resource or increasing the timeout period.

- Insufficient permissions: The necessary permissions are not present to create a resource. To resolve this, check your AWS Identity and Access Management (IAM) permissions and the service role used by CloudFormation.

- Resource Limit Exceeded: The resources needed to create the stack exceed resource limits. To tackle this problem, you may need to request an increase in your service quota or optimize your resources.

3.3. Traversing Log Files

AWS CloudFormation™ creates a series of log files in Amazon CloudWatch™ Logs, where detailed stack operations are kept. These become invaluable tools in identifying the cause of a failure. Often, the AWS CloudFormation™ console's Events tab does not provide enough insight into complex issues. With Amazon CloudWatch™ Logs, the veil is drawn back, revealing more detailed stack events to provide a better understanding of where things veered off course.

Logs provide significant in-depth knowledge such as the precise timing of each event, the specific resources involved, and, critically, more detailed error messages. Understanding might require a bit of sifting, as log files capture a lot of noise, not all of which pertains to the issue at hand.

3.4. Stack Creation and Rollback Handling

While a failed stack creation generally leads to AWS CloudFormation™ automatically deleting the stack, the same is not true for stack updates. When a stack update fails, AWS CloudFormation™ attempts to roll back the successful updates made and return the stack to its original state, unless you have explicitly set a policy preventing that.

This process can itself fail under certain circumstances, and the rollback might not be able to return the stack to its initial form, thus rendering the stack status as `UPDATE_ROLLBACK_FAILED`. In such an event, CloudFormation offers options like continuing the rollback, skipping resources that may have caused the rollback failure (using AWS CLI), or even deleting the stack entirely.

It's important to note that during the automatic rollback process, all the resources created as a part of the stack creation or update process are deleted, barring the ones for which the Deletion Policy or RetainPolicy has been set. In such cases, CloudFormation retains the resources as specified.

3.5. Debugging Through AWS CloudFormation Drift Detection

AWS CloudFormation Drift Detection is another feature that helps identify the deviations between stack resources and their current configurations in AWS. It compares the current stack configuration and the one recorded in the AWS CloudFormation™ console after the last successfully completed stack operation.

When resource configurations do not match, a 'drifted' state is reported on the CloudFormation console, notifying you of the discrepancies. This feature fosters visibility into configuration variance and ensures configuration management maintaining accurate infrastructure visibility.

The technicalities surrounding CloudFormation Stack Creation failures are indeed vast and complex. Identifying these failures is your first step towards resolution. Familiarity with the common failure types, delving into the error messages and logs and understanding stack creation and rollback processing will help you mitigate these issues more effectively. But remember, the best debugging tool is still a keen understanding of your system's structure and a rigorous thought process. In our subsequent chapters, we will delve into strategies to rectify these failures and preventive measures to avoid similar issues in the future.

Chapter 4. Decoding Error Messages in Stack Failures

Understanding the error messages in stack failures can go a long way in resolving the issues quickly and effectively. Negative outcomes, failures, or errors are not the end in themselves. Instead, they are vital intersections where we can pause, observe, understand, and improve. A key to resolving any failure is understanding exactly what went wrong, and in the complex domain of AWS CloudFormation, error messages provide that crucial insight.

4.1. Recognizing The Structure Of Error Messages

Error messages in AWS CloudFormation have a distinct structure that consists of detailed information about the error's cause, location, and possible resolution. It typically has a descriptive error message, error type, resource type impacted and detailed facts to aid troubleshooting. Understanding this structure can help you find the relevant information quickly and move one step closer to resolution.

However, the messages may sometimes fall short of providing a comprehensive explanation of the problem due to their generic nature. Reading between the lines and interpreting the implications of these messages become necessary to decode the error effectively.

4.2. The Most Common Error Message Scenarios

To help you understand what sort of error messages you might encounter while working with AWS CloudFormation, a few of the most common scenarios encountered include:

- Resource creation limits exceeded: AWS has set limits on the resources you can create, and if your stack tries to create more than the allowed number, you'll run into this error. The error message precisely points at the resource causing the problem. Resolution often involves requesting a limit raise or adjusting the stack to comply with the limits.

- Insufficient permissions: When AWS CloudFormation does not have the necessary permissions to perform an action, an IAM-related error message is returned. Resolve this by adjusting the permissions associated with the IAM role.

- Conditional check failed: This error signifies that some condition mentioned in your stack template has failed. The error message helps identify which check failed and what conditions led to this failure.

- Parameters validation failed: Signifies that the parameters provided while creating stack failed the validation checks. The error message will provide details on which parameters failed and why.

- Dependency errors: Indicates that a resource that another resource depends on failed to create or delete. It's solved by troubleshooting the dependent resource mentioned in the error message.

4.3. Decoding The Language Of Error Messages

Let's delve further into how AWS CloudFormation communicates its errors.

- ROLLBACK_IN_PROGRESS: Implies that AWS CloudFormation is rolling back to the previous stack configuration because the stack creation or modification failed.

- ROLLBACK_FAILED: Signals that the rollback operation itself has failed. AWS CloudFormation could not revert to the previous stack configuration, leaving the stack in an unstable state.

- UPDATE_ROLLBACK_FAILED: AWS CloudFormation failed to roll back an update operation. You need to manually fix the issues that caused the failed rollback.

- CREATE_FAILED or DELETE_FAILED: Implies the operation to create or delete a specific resource failed.

It can be challenging to precisely understand these without contextual error messages. Make sure to explore the "Events" tab of the CloudFormation console for detailed error messages associated with these statuses.

4.4. Considerations For Problematic Resources

You'll need to deal with specific error scenarios where certain resources are either problematic to work with or leave behind artifacts when a stack fails to create successfully.

For instance, the AWS::Route53::HostedZone resource does not get deleted even after a stack is deleted because of this resource. You would need to manually delete records in it before it can be deleted.

Also, be aware of the circular dependency problem where resources reference each other indirectly creating a resource loop. AWS CloudFormation returns an error if it detects a loop in the resource dependency chain.

4.5. Conclusion

Decoding error messages effectively can expedite the process of resolving stack creation failures significantly. Remember, error messages are your friend for they provide you insight into what exactly went wrong. It's all about addressing these signals in a structured manner for swift and effective resolution.

Every developer engaged in the world of cloud computing will bump into these challenges at some point in time. Armed with a deeper understanding and a distinct approach to such errors, you can steer your stack creations to successful conclusions more quickly and confidently.

Chapter 5. Troubleshooting Techniques: A Deep Dive

Understanding the challenges faced during the creation of AWS CloudFormation Stacks, and the solutions for these problems, requires a profound comprehension of several facets. In this chapter, we'll delve deep into several troubleshooting techniques, footnoting key areas with expert suggestions and examples.

5.1. Identifying Stack Failures

Knowing where to begin diagnosing the root cause of stack failure is the first step of the troubleshooting process. AWS CloudFormation explicitly notifies you whenever a resource fails to create or delete, which you can find in the `Stack events` section of the AWS CloudFormation console. Be sure to compare the listed failures with the AWS CloudFormation error codes documentation.

Besides, you can activate AWS CloudTrail to keep an audit log of the API operations made on CloudFormation. The `errorCode` and `errorMessage` details provide more context on the particularities of the issue.

5.2. Deciphering Error Messages

AWS CloudFormation displays error messages if a function fails. Understanding these messages is paramount. Most of the messages quote the AWS CloudFormation template component that has failed, which accelerates your bug-hunting process.

When an error occurs, go through the `Status reason` field under the `Events` tab. But not all error messages are as plain and straightforward as one would hope. In such scenarios, consider looking at service-specific troubleshooting guides in the AWS documentation or seeking guidance on forum platforms like Stack Overflow.

5.3. Service Quotas

Infringement of service quotas is a common reason for stack creation failure in CloudFormation. AWS services have stipulated quotas, aka limits, for each region, and breaching this quota would result in failure. To fix this, you either need to delete existing resources or request an increase in the quota by creating a service limit increase case with AWS Support. To avoid such issues in the future, it's recommended to monitor your quota usage regularly using AWS Service Quotas or AWS Trusted Advisor.

5.4. Network Configuration

One often overlooked aspect during stack creation is the network configuration. If there's an error linked to IAM service roles, VPC, Subnets, Security Groups, or associated resources, it can cause the stack to fail. Review the respective details - like ensuring proper permissions for IAM roles, checking IP Tenancy or confirming if the Security Groups allow the necessary inbound and outbound access.

5.5. Utilizing AWS Management Console

The AWS Management Console is an incredibly effective tool for troubleshooting AWS CloudFormation template syntax and runtime errors. It lets you preview changes to a stack and diagnose issues prior to executing changes.

The 'estimate template cost' feature gives you a rough estimate of costs associated with the utilized AWS services, allowing you to plan budget accordingly. In addition, the 'view in designer' feature provides a well-laid graphical representation of your template to better understand dependencies and configuration.

5.6. Maximizing AWS CLI and SDKs

AWS Command Line Interface (CLI) and SDKs can help debug the issues through commands and scripts. They can provide a wealth of details and context about the encountered errors, which can be especially beneficial if multiple resources are at play.

However, bear in mind that effective diagnosis with CLI and SDKs presupposes a fair amount of familiarity with AWS jargon and operations. Begin your journey with these advanced tools gradually, familiarize yourself with basic commands first before delving into complex scripts.

5.7. Resource Creation Timing

Surprisingly, the timing of resource creation can also be a contributing factor to stack failure. The service may take longer than expected to bring a resource up and running, causing the AWS CloudFormation to time out.

Take note of the `WaitCondition` and `CreationPolicy` attributes. They allow your stack to pause for a specified period or until a specific condition is met before creating the next resource.

5.8. Deleting Stuck Stacks

When a stack operation fails, you might end up with a stuck stack. In such scenarios, make sure to diagnose the cause first and then attempt to delete it. If deletion failed, you can either delete the individual resources manually or retain the resources while deleting the stack by specifying `RetainResources` in `DeleteStack`.

5.9. Leveraging AWS Support and Whitepapers

Last but not least, AWS provides exceptional support in troubleshooting CloudFormation failures. AWS Support Center, Developer Forum, and knowledge-embedded whitepapers are just a few avenues to exploit.

Furthermore, consider investing in AWS Support Plans. A well-selected support plan can provide you not only faster access to cloud support engineers, but also 24/7 access to a concierge support team.

CloudFormation stack creation failures can be daunting initially, but with a well-defined approach to identifying and resolving these issues, you transform a failure into a learning opportunity. Remember, troubleshooting is an acquired skill, and the deeper you dive into it, the better you get.

In the end, AWS CloudFormation is an immensely powerful service that, if navigated correctly, can significantly streamline your resource management, giving you a major leg-up in your cloud journey. Just remember, every failure is a stepping stone to mastery. Commit your expertise to learning from these slip-ups rather than avoiding them.

Chapter 6. Resolving CloudFormation Service Limit Issues

One of the major hindrances that users face while dealing with CloudFormation is exceeding the prescribed service limits. Service limits defined by AWS are basically safety mechanisms that prevent users from using resources indiscriminately. In the case of CloudFormation, these are set on a per-region basis. However, this restriction can often lead to stack creation failure.

6.1. Understanding CloudFormation Service Limits

Service limit is a protection measure by AWS to ensure optimal performance and prevent abuse. If you exceed these limits, AWS may return an error message. In AWS CloudFormation, these limitations pertain to the number of stacks you can create simultaneously, the fraction of the desired capacity for auto scaling, among others. Given the nuances of these limitations and the potential for unintended overconsumption, a deep understanding is pivotal for effective operation.

Although service limits are primarily a protection measure as they prevent the user from unintentionally exhausting resources, their excessive efficiency can sometimes cause disruptions. A common issue is stack creation failure when the stack limit is exceeded. This is a scenario where CloudFormation rejects your stack creation request because you have reached the maximum number of allowable stacks.

6.2. How to Identify CloudFormation Service Limit Issues

You may not always receive an explicit notification indicating that you've crossed the service limit. When stack creation fails due to service limit, typically, AWS CloudFormation displays an error message 'Rate exceeded.'

To identify a service limit issue, you need to verify CloudFormation event logs. If CloudFormation fails to create a stack, it will place the stack in the ROLLBACK_COMPLETE status, but with a thorough inspection of the stack events, you can determine if service limits were truly the cause.

Keep in mind that the signs of service limit issues are not always obvious. If you see resources failing to create without a clear explanation, this could be an indicator of service limit problems.

6.3. Working around CloudFormation Service Limit Issues

Preventing service limit issues is often simpler than fixing them. However, if you face stack creation failures due to service limits, you can follow these steps:

1. Request an increase in service limits from the AWS Management Console. Detail your requirements and the AWS Support will increase your limits.

2. Delete unused stacks. This frees up resources to create a new stack, aiding you to verify if the issue was actually due to service limits.

3. Use AWS Trusted Advisor to check your service limit usage. It

helps manage your AWS environment by providing real-time guidance.

4. Increase the throttle settings of your AWS SDK client. A delay in the rate of API calls to AWS services might prevent the 'Rate exceeded' error.

5. Use exponential backoff in AWS SDKs. This strategy helps manage the frequency at which your application makes requests.

Remember, if any of the above steps resolve the issue, service limits were likely the cause.

6.4. Avoiding Future CloudFormation Service Limit Issues

To prevent such problems in the future, be proactive in managing and monitoring service limits:

1. Constantly monitor your AWS quotas with AWS Service Quotas.

2. Set up CloudWatch Alarms for approaching limits, which can trigger Amazon SNS topics when breached.

3. If feasible, spread your resources across multiple AWS accounts or regions.

4. Implement infrastructure as code in an efficient manner using AWS CloudFormation nested stacks.

5. Use AWS Trusted Advisor or third-party tools to continuously monitor and manage service usage.

By maintaining a vigilant eye upon your AWS resources, and intelligently planning and partitioning your operations, you can effectively navigate around CloudFormation Service Limit issues. This can ensure a seamless, unobstructed workflow while leveraging the full potential of AWS CloudFormation services.

In conclusion, although service limits in AWS CloudFormation can be a hurdle, with a sound understanding, vigilance and effective resource management, they can be managed. The key is to stay mindful of your usage and make regular assessments of your AWS environment. Whether you are a seasoned cloud practitioner or a novice stepping into the arena, recognition of these challenges and strategies to combat them will equip you well for your journey with AWS CloudFormation.

Chapter 7. Dealing with Insufficient IAM Permissions

Let's start tackling one of the most widespread issues that cause a CloudFormation Stack creation failure: Insufficient Identity and Access Management (IAM) permissions.

IAM is fundamentally an Amazon Web Services (AWS) mechanism used to manage resources securely. It helps maintain control over the authentication and authorization processes of your AWS resources. Though IAM offers better control, it can bring about trickiness to your CloudFormation Stack creation should there be insufficient permissions. When the permissions are not aptly set, you land on the dreaded "Insufficient IAM permissions" error, which puts an abrupt full stop to your Stack creation.

Scenario Analysis ===

Let's look at a real-world instance to better grasp this issue. Imagine you're setting up an AWS CloudFormation Stack to create an Amazon Simple Storage Service (S3) bucket. When the stack attempts to run the CreateBucket action but doesn't have adequate IAM permissions for this task, the creation fails, triggering the said error. So, you see now that fumbling around IAM permissions can lead to the potential roadblock in your journey to configure your preferred AWS resources.

Clarifying the Error ===

AWS states an "Access Denied" error message when IAM permissions are insufficient. Though it might appear as a vague delineation and hindrance, it serves as an effective security measure by AWS to prevent providing more information than required that could assist malicious actors.

Yet, experienced eyes could identify the part of the CloudFormation Stack that was blocked due to inadequate permissions, as the error message also shows the specific API call that led to the failure. Notably, in cases where the stack's rollback feature is enabled, it can help identify the resources that were not formulated due to this error.

Understanding IAM Roles Permissions ===

IAM roles play a pivotal role in granting permissions. Each IAM role holds an associated policy, which concisely lists the permissions the role has imbued. It can either be:

1. Directly associated with a user

2. Assumed by users when needed, to perform particular tasks

IAM roles associated with CloudFormation operate in two major ways:

1. Service role: Leveraged during the stack operation to create, update, or delete resources

2. Execution role: Granted to the CloudFormation service to make API calls to the required AWS services

Both roles bear different responsibilities; hence the permissions need to be meticulously assigned, thus making them able to perform their intended actions.

Remedying Insufficient Permissions ===

To mend the issue of 'Insufficient IAM permissions,' put these steps into action:

1. First, cross-check if the intended action aligns with the IAM role's in-place policy. Investigate the permissions provided to the IAM roles for the CloudFormation Stack during its creation or update.

Is there a specific 'deny' statement related to the failed action in the IAM policy? Or is any other rule causing a conflict?

2. More often than not, you might find an explicit deny policy, overriding other policy statements. In that case, you need to adjust the IAM policies accordingly.

3. The AWS Management Console, AWS CLI, or AWS SDKs can be wielded to modify IAM policies. Once that's sorted, attempt to recreate or update the stack.

4. If the issue persists, delve deeper to study each IAM policy and understand which action of which service is being denied or not included. Make sure that all needed services are incorporated into the IAM policy.

5. In doing so, it is likely that you might introduce overly permissive policies, causing a potential security threat. Thus, ensure that the IAM policies uphold the least priviliege principle, granting minimum permissions required for the users to perform their tasks. Proper adherence to this principle minimizes security risks substantially.

Determining and Setting Proper Permissions ===

Determining the proper IAM permissions for your CloudFormation stack depends upon the AWS services you intend to configure within the stack. It also relies on the specific actions that are to be performed on them. Abrupt issues can spring up if you are unaware of the required permissions, so it's imperative to painstakingly understand the services and required permissions when you design your CloudFormation stack.

AWS Managed Policies for CloudFormation can be a good starting point to set up permissions. AWS has two distinct managed policies that can assist you:

1. AWSCloudFormationReadOnlyAccess

2. AWSCloudFormationFullAccess

While the former provides read-only access to AWS services during stack updates, the latter offers full access to AWS services that CloudFormation could potentially interact with. Leveraging these managed policies, you piece together a well-constructed policy that aligns with your needs and abides by the least privileges rule.

To wrap up, CloudFormation is an invaluable service provided by AWS that automates infrastructure provisioning and management. However, it requires careful navigation around IAM permissions to ensure smooth execution. Insufficient permissions could lead to CloudFormation Stack creation failures, setting back your progress substantially. However, with a clear understanding of IAM roles and crafting appropriate IAM policies, you can bypass the "Insufficient IAM permissions" error, advancing your CloudFormation operations without hitches.

This exhaustive account of dealing with insufficient IAM permissions admittedly begins sounding complex, but as you work your way through it, the intricacies start to unravel. Remember, patience is vital, and so is an in-depth understanding of the roles and services in use. Here's hoping this guide proves to be your faithful companion in your CloudFormation journey!

Chapter 8. Rectifying Template File Issues: A Practical Approach

The oversight or mismanagement of template files can often result in CloudFormation Stack creation failure. The underlying problem could potentially stem from a wide array of issues, including syntactical errors, violations of defined limits, and incorrect references, among others.

8.1. Troubleshooting Syntactical Errors

The examination of stack creation failure should always start with a thorough check performed on the template file for possible syntactical errors. Amazon CloudFormation relies heavily on the specific syntax of JSON or YAML to function correctly. Even a tiny typographical error could disrupt the stack's deployment.

If the AWS Management Console is being used, a handy tool is the built-in Template Designer. It allows you to visualize your template and can quickly identify incorrect syntax. If you're using a textual editor, there are linters available for JSON and YAML that will perform this function. Always double-check the colons, commas, or brackets before proceeding.

8.2. Managing Limits Violations

Amazon CloudFormation sets certain service limits, and any template that breaches these constraints would inevitably fail. To avoid this, stay informed about the current limitations for both stack and regional level resources.

Using the AWS service 'Service Quotas' allows you to view and manage your quotas easily and to request quota increases for adjustable quotas in one central location. Also, nested stacks can help you organize your AWS CloudFormation stacks and reduce your stack count.

8.3. Rectifying Incorrect References

A common mistake during AWS CloudFormation template creation is using incorrect references. Whether it is references to other resources or improperly defined outputs, these can cause the stack creation to fail. AWS offers the intrinsic function `Fn::Ref` for proper referencing. It is crucial to ensure that `Fn::Ref` is being used appropriately, and that referenced resources and outputs have been defined and initialized before use.

If AWS CloudFormation returns an error message stating that a resource mentioned in your template doesn't exist, verify that it does exist in the AWS CloudFormation stack and that you referenced it correctly in your template.

8.4. Ensuring Resource Availability

If your template refers to resources that do not have the required availability, it may result in a stack creation failure. Check the availability of IAM roles, Lambda functions, EC2 instances, and other resources specific to AWS services before pointing to them in your template.

Also, when creating IAM resources, AWS CloudFormation may return a 'CREATE_FAILED' error if it doesn't have the necessary permissions. Therefore, be sure to provide appropriate permissions if your stack includes IAM resources.

8.5. Optimizing Helper Scripts

Helper scripts, such as AWS::CloudFormation::Init and metadata, when not optimized correctly, can also lead to stack failure. It is noteworthy to mention that EC2 instances have metadata which AWS CloudFormation can utilize.

Inefficiently managed or incorrectly called helper scripts may hamper the working of metadata leading to failure in the execution of desired tasks and subsequently stack creation. Always ensure that they are correctly called upon, defined, and are performing optimally.

8.6. Debugging Custom Logic Errors

AWS CloudFormation allows creating AWS Lambda-backed custom resources in your CloudFormation stack. This gives you the freedom to incorporate various functionalities or specific tasks on AWS resources that CloudFormation does not natively support.

However, along with the flexibility of Lambda functions, there is an increased responsibility to manage them correctly. Any mismanaged custom logic can lead to stack creation failure. Make sure to invoke these Lambda functions appropriately and handle all the necessary conditions.

In conclusion, rectifying template file issues can be daunting due to the technical complexity associated with it. However, adopting a systematic approach in diagnosing the situation makes troubleshooting a more manageable task. Recognise that a failed CloudFormation stack is not the end but an opportunity for improvement. With a bit of diligence and the best practices outlined above, you can bypass the pitfalls and complex situations to ensure flawless stack creation in AWS CloudFormation.

Chapter 9. Preventing Future Stack Creation Failures

Formulating adequate preventive measures against future CloudFormation Stack creation failures necessitates a multifaceted approach. This comprehensive plan will encompass understanding stack creation workflow, rigorous template checking, diligent parameter management, error loop avoidance, enforcing IAM permissions, and logging best practices among several others. Let's delve into these strategies in detail.

9.1. Understanding Stack Creation Workflow

The first essential preventive measure is to fully comprehend CloudFormation stack creation workflow. Every resource is treated as a stack in CloudFormation, and an understanding of how these stacks are created will give you a head start in identifying potential issues early on. Remember that when a stack is executed, AWS CloudFormation first validates the template, followed by checking that you have enough permissions to build resources. It then proceeds to create and configure AWS resources, maintaining the order defined in the template.

Enlightening oneself about the inner workings of this should give scope for better preparedness and allow for more effective preventive measures. AWS's provision of a thorough visualization of the stack creation process can provide significant aid in understanding the process while embedding this knowledge in your cloud computing practices.

9.2. Rigorous Template Checking

Conducting comprehensive template checks prior to utilization can help in preventing failure in stack creation. AWS CloudFormation uses templates to create resources, and any error in these can lead to failure. Therefore, both structurally validating your templates and verifying the included content against AWS guidelines will prevent failure from flawed parameters or values.

Consider using Automatic Template Generation for stacks, provided by AWS CloudFormation. These are invaluable aids for double-checking especially complex templates, and can even auto-correct minor mistakes, ensuring your stack creation goes smoothly.

9.3. Diligent Parameter Management

Failing to manage parameters proactively can lead to issues in stack creation. Clear documentation and regular maintenance of parameters, with their corresponding values, relationships, and dependencies, are also an essential part of prevention.

Implementing a parameter management routine can help ensure all parameter data are up-to-date and accurate. To be specific, you should ensure that parameters align with the expectations set by AWS. A wrongly specified parameter can lead to AWS rejecting the stack creation request, leading to failure.

9.4. Error Loop Avoidance

Preventing error loops is perhaps one of the most effective strategies against future failures. Loop errors generally occur when a failed stack rollback is retried and fails again. This cycle can repeat multiple times and cause numerous failures, having a profound impact on deployment and application functioning.

To break this loop, avoid using the 'Always' option for failure handling in Stack Policy. Opt for 'DoNothing' or 'Rollback' instead. Also, monitoring the stack status regularly allows early error detection and helps in breaking failure loops.

9.5. Enforcing IAM Permissions

Ensuring appropriate permissions can prevent failures due to inadequate or incorrect Identity and Access Management (IAM) rights. In CloudFormation, every operation against a stack corresponds to a unique IAM role, and it's crucial that all relevant roles have the necessary permissions.

Consistent testing of IAM roles, combined with the audit logging process, can shed light on permissions issues before stack creation, thereby allowing for preemptive mitigation. Also, practicing the Principle of Least Privilege, i.e., providing only the privileges necessary for a task, greatly reduces chances of failure.

9.6. Logging Best Practices

Adhering to best practices in logging aids in the identification of potential threats to stack creation, allowing for proactive issue resolution. Capacity to analyze logs helps in identifying patterns that may be indicative of potential failures. AWS CloudWatch is a good tool for collecting and tracking metrics, monitoring log files, setting alarms, and automatically reacting to changes in AWS resources.

As a rule of thumb, always log all successful and unsuccessful attempts at stack creation, along with any error messages. Also, monitor AWS' resource-level APIs via CloudTrail for additional insights and patterns.

While these preventive measures greatly reduce the chance of future stack creation failures, the broad and dynamic nature of cloud computing means that new challenges are always emerging. By understanding and implementing these practices, it translates to fewer stack creation failures, saving both time and resources, leading to optimized cloud operations.

Chapter 10. Best Practices for Effective CloudFormation Usage

Technological advancements in cloud platforms like AWS have enabled organizations to achieve new feats in scalability, data management, and security. Among the array of services offered by AWS, one tool that stands out for its robust functionality is AWS CloudFormation. Yet, it's effectiveness entirely depends on proper utilization and sound practices. Below we delve into the best practices that users should adhere to attain an effective CloudFormation usage.

10.1. Understanding AWS CloudFormation

AWS CloudFormation service lets you model and provision AWS resources as per your requirements. It utilizes a text file to emulate and provision all the resources needed for your applications across all regions and accounts. This file serves as the single source of truth enabling you to manage your infrastructure in a predictive and declarative manner.

CloudFormation service lets you use various programming languages or a simple text file to model and provision, in an automated and secure manner, all the resources for your applications. However, it can sometimes be a tricky endeavor, especially if the best practices are not embraced.

10.2. Hand Crafted Stacks versus Programmatically Defined Stacks

When setting out on your CloudFormation journey, you will encounter two principal approaches to defining stacks: hand-crafted and programmatically.

Hand-crafted stacks require manual efforts to edit and maintain the YAML/JSON scripts. Although it offers precise control over stack resources, it can pose a significant burden when your application grows in complexity.

On the other hand, programmatically defined stacks are created using developer-friendly languages such as TypeScript or Python. These stacks dynamically generate the CloudFormation script using AWS Cloud Development Kit (AWS CDK). Benefit being, re-usability of components, and ease of maintenance.

Explicitly defining all of your infrastructure directly in JSON or YAML files can quickly become laborious and error-prone. Hence, gradually, programmatically defined stacks are gaining momentum and have become an emerging norm.

10.3. Utilizing AWS Managed Services

AWS Managed services reduce the operational overhead by abstracting the infrastructural details. These services manage the security, compliance, and provisioning of resources in the background, freeing up developers to concentrate on more prominent issues. When dealing with CloudFormation, it is a good practice to leverage AWS managed services like DynamoDB, Lambda, etc., instead of creating your resources.

10.4. Laying Out Your Directories Correctly

Proper directory layout is crucial in the CloudFormation scenario. Here's a recommended way to structure your directories for clarity and ease of updates:

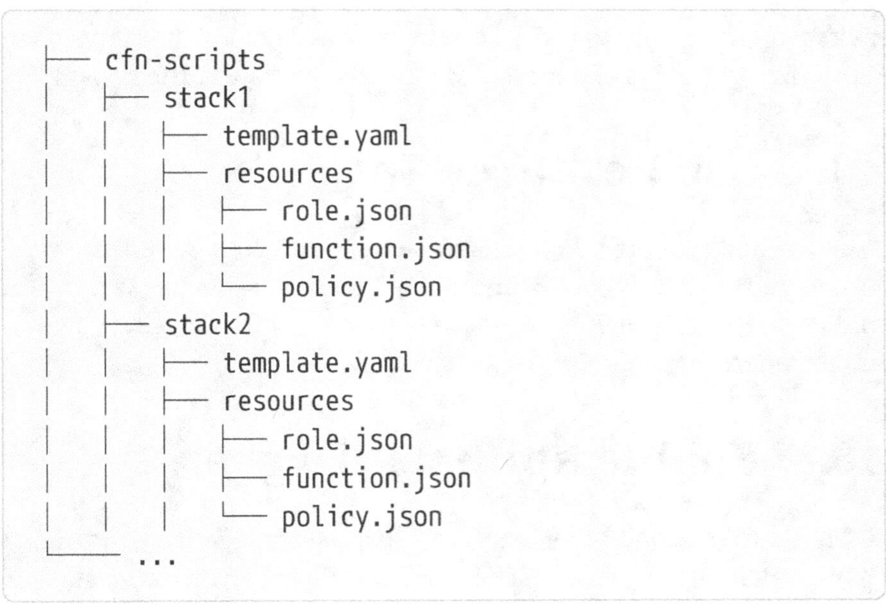

10.5. Break Down Your Stacks

Regardless of the size of your application, breaking down the CloudFormation stack into smaller, manageable, logical units can be beneficial, allowing easier troubleshooting, and reducing the risk of exceeding CloudFormation service quotas.

10.6. Embrace Immutable Infrastructure

Immutable infrastructure reduces inconsistencies and boosts recoverability by treating servers and other infrastructure components as "disposable." Rather than altering an existing environment, new servers or resources are built, the traffic is switched over, and the old resources are deleted. This approach minimizes variables and increases the effectiveness of the system.

10.7. Use Resource Tags

Resource tags enable you to assign metadata to your AWS resources. By tagging resources, you can quickly identify, organize, search for, and report on specific assets based on their purpose, owner, environment, or other criteria.

10.8. Enable Rollback Triggers

Rollback triggers automatically roll back stack deployments when CloudWatch alarms are breached. Stack rollback ensures the stack is in a stable state if things go south during a deployment. It mitigates the impact of failed deployments, reducing downtime and helping maintain continuity of service.

10.9. Implement Nested Stacks

Nested stack allows you to create, update, or delete a collection of related resources as a single unit. Refactor your CloudFormation stack into nested stacks makes it more modular and easier to manage.

10.10. Monitor Stack Changes

Keeping track of stack changes ensure that any unwanted alterations or errors can be dealt with swiftly. AWS provides CloudFormation StackSets for overseeing stack changes from a single-touchpoint.

10.11. Enforce Stack Policies

Stack policies protect critical stack resources from unintentional updates. Specifying a stack policy will restrain the operations that can be executed on designated resources, enhancing the security and stability of your application.

Thus, effective CloudFormation usage involves a considerable amount of best practices and thorough knowledge of AWS norms. It's about moving forward with a clear understanding of your cloud vision and fine-tuning your approach as per the business requirements. AWS CloudFormation, if used judiciously, is indeed a powerful tool to keep your infrastructure organized, secure, and scalable.

Chapter 11. Success Stories: Resolving CloudFormation Challenges and Failures

When it comes to working with AWS CloudFormation, everyone has their share of stories where they faced challenges and overcame failures. Let's delve into a few detailed accounts of these real-life challenges and their solutions, hoping they enlighten you on possible pitfalls and optimal ways to subvert them.

11.1. Troubleshooting Stack Rollback Failures

Rollback failures can be a tough nut to crack, and if not handled properly, they can snowball into a bigger issue. In one particular instance, a backend team at a tech startup encountered stack rollback failures during the launch of a new project. Surprisingly, CloudFormation did not provide an explicit error message, which aggravated the situation.

After several debugging sessions, the team discovered their error. The issue stemmed from a DynamoDB table creation which had a GlobalSecondaryIndex. The Index had an attribute that was mistakenly defined in non-existing resources. The solution came in two phases:

1. Rectifying the DynamoDB table definition by pointing the Index attribute to the correct resources.

2. Adding explicit `DependsOn` attributes to ensure the necessary resources are created before the DynamoDB table.

The team also made two essential improvements to their practices.

First, they invested more time in pre-launch testing, especially within each individual stack's resources. Second, they utilized `cfn-lint`, a CloudFormation linter which validates templates and catches errors, including resource and property references, before a stack launch.

11.2. Understanding the Low-frequency Errors

Sometimes, "rare" errors can occur that are less understood due to their infrequency. An e-commerce company faced a sporadic stack creation failure due to "Rate exceeded" errors. They were in a region where there was a low limit on control plane operations, and during peak traffic, they occasionally hit the AWS-managed API request throttle.

To resolve this, the team:

1. Reached out to AWS support, who increased their account's limit per region.

2. Implemented exponential backoffs and retries for their retry logic in AWS SDKs to handle request throttling.

Moreover, they launched a time-series monitoring system that observes their AWS API usage frequency, helping them anticipate similar issues more effectively in the future.

11.3. Navigating Cross-Stack References

A large enterprise tasked with managing multiple stacks faced challenges with cross-stack dependencies. Particularly, they had a hard time referencing a security group created in one stack from another stack.

The team's way around this issue comprised:

1. Using AWS CloudFormation Stack outputs to expose the security group's ID from the creating stack.

2. Introducing AWS CloudFormation Imports within the depending stack to bring in the exposed output from the creating stack.

This allowed the stacks to successfully reference the security group, thus resolving the issue. This practice drove them to establish a standardized naming convention for their Stack outputs, making cross-stack references efficient across all their projects.

11.4. Ensuring Desirable State After Failure

A software-as-a-service company had a unique challenge: maintaining a desirable state after a CloudFormation stack update failure. In an unfortunate event of update failure, they were required to handle changes manually but found it cumbersome.

The team confronted this problem by:

1. Setting the `StackPolicy` during initial stack creation, which by default allows updates to all resources.

2. Modifying the `StackPolicy` during update operations to prevent resources from being accidentally deleted.

This approach ensured that resources weren't mistakenly deleted during stack update failures, enabling the team to maintain a desirable state. This resulted in lowering the time spent rectifying Stack update failures.

11.5. Encrypting Sensitive Data in Transit

A fintech startup was dealing with sensitive financial data and needed to ensure that their data in-transit was encrypted while using CloudFormation. By implementing AWS Key Management System (KMS), they encrypted their data from potential eavesdroppers.

Here's how they managed:

1. Generated a customer-managed key using KMS.

2. Referenced the KMS key in their S3 bucket policies, allowing only objects encrypted by the key to be stored.

3. Updated their applications to include the KMS key during the upload of any object onto S3.

By doing so, they assured their data was always encrypted in transit, providing strong protection for sensitive financial data and enhancing trust among their customers.

Unearthing these stories draws light to the multifaceted nature of issues that one may encounter while dealing with CloudFormation. By understanding these situations and their solutions, you can better position yourself to handle CloudFormation failures differently and more proficiently in the future.